Pebble®

Polar Animals

Arctic Hares

by Helen Frost

Consulting Editor: Gail Saunders-Smith, PhD

Consultant: Brian M. Barnes, Director
Institute of Arctic Biology
University of Alaska, Fairbanks

Capstone
press®

Mankato, Minnesota

j599.328
FRO

Pebble Books are published by Capstone Press,
151 Good Counsel Drive, P.O. Box 669, Mankato, Minnesota 56002.
www.capstonepress.com

1 2 3 4 5 6 11 10 09 08 07 06

Library of Congress Cataloging-in-Publication Data
Frost, Helen.
   Arctic hares / by Helen Frost.
   p. cm.—(Pebble books. Polar animals)
   Summary: "Simple text and photographs present arctic hares, where they live,
and what they do"—Provided by publisher.
   Includes bibliographical references and index.
   ISBN-13: 978-0-7368-4243-3 (hardcover)
   ISBN-10: 0-7368-4243-8 (hardcover)
   1. Arctic hare—Juvenile literature. I. Title. II. Series.
QL737.L32F73 2007
599.32'8—dc22   2004026894

Note to Parents and Teachers

The Polar Animals set supports national science standards related
to life science. This book describes and illustrates arctic hares.
The images support early readers in understanding the text. The
repetition of words and phrases helps early readers learn new
words. This book also introduces early readers to subject-specific
vocabulary words, which are defined in the Glossary section. Early
readers may need assistance to read some words and to use the
Table of Contents, Glossary, Read More, Internet Sites, and Index
sections of the book.

Table of Contents

What Are Arctic Hares?

Arctic hares are mammals.
Hares look like rabbits.

Arctic hares have
gray and brown fur
in the summer.
Their fur turns white
in the winter.

land where arctic hares live

Where Arctic Hares Live

Arctic hares live
in the far north.
They live on the tundra.

Body Parts

Arctic hares have
long claws.
They dig through snow
to find plants to eat.

Arctic hares have
long ears with black tips.
They listen for predators.

Arctic hares have
strong legs.
They run fast to get away
from predators.

What Arctic Hares Do

Arctic hares can
stay very still.
Their white fur is hard
to see in the snow.

Arctic hares sometimes live in groups.
They watch for predators.

Arctic hares make burrows in the snow. They rest in their burrows during the day.

Glossary

burrow—a tunnel or hole in the ground made or used by an animal; arctic hares make burrows in the snow.

claw—a hard, curved nail on the foot of an animal

hare—a mammal that is like a large rabbit, with long, strong back legs

mammal—a warm-blooded animal that has a backbone; mammals have fur or hair; female mammals feed milk to their young.

predator—an animal that hunts other animals for food; wolves, snowy owls, and arctic foxes are predators that hunt and eat arctic hares.

tundra—a flat, cold area without trees; the ground stays frozen in the tundra for most of the year.

Read More

Lindeen, Carol K. *Life in a Polar Region.* Living in a Biome. Mankato, Minn.: Capstone Press, 2004.

Longenecker, Theresa. *Who Grows Up in the Snow?: A Book about Snow Animals and Their Offspring.* Minneapolis: Picture Window Books, 2003.

Internet Sites

FactHound offers a safe, fun way to find Internet sites related to this book. All of the sites on FactHound have been researched by our staff.

Here's how:

1. Visit *www.facthound.com*

2. Choose your grade level.

3. Type in this book ID **0736842438** for age-appropriate sites. You may also browse subjects by clicking on letters, or by clicking on pictures and words.

4. Click on the **Fetch It** button.

FactHound will fetch the best sites for you!

Index

Word Count: 117
Grade: 1
Early-Intervention Level: 14

Editorial Credits
Martha E. H. Rustad, editor; Patrick D. Dentinger, designer; Wanda Winch, photo
  researcher; Scott Thoms, photo editor

Photo Credits
Bruce Coleman Inc./Rolf Kopfle, 1
Cheryl A. Ertelt, 14
Corbis/Kennan Ward, 16; Staffan Widstrand, 8
Houserstock/Dave G. Houser, 4, 12
Minden Pictures/Jim Brandenburg, 10, 18
Peter Arnold, Inc./S. J. Krasemann, 6
SeaPics/Michael S. Nolan, cover
Superstock/age fotostock, 20